UNCK
YOUR
YEAR

*A Weekly Unplanner and
Self-Care Activity Book
to Manage Your Anxiety, Depression,
Anger, Triggers, and Freak-Outs*

FAITH G. HARPER, PhD, LPC-S, ACS, ACN

MICROCOSM PUBLISHING
Portland, OR

INTRODUCTION

Hey there, superfriends!

One thing we hear all the time is how much y'all love worksheets and workbooks. (Your 4th grade teachers should all be hella proud.)

But we know what you're really telling us is that you know you have work to do. I mean, the world is full of people who have work to do, but if you are holding this book in your hand you are the type of person who takes complete responsibility for that fact. Even if 90% of your work is finding ways to deal with all the people who are refusing to do their own work.

We can't go back in time and make things magically better. But we can stand up and say:

It stops here.
It stops with me.
I choose healing. So the world can see healing is possible.

Though, of course, that work isn't easy. Despite what a lot of pseudoscience gurus say, real change takes continued, concentrated effort. Easy and instantaneous is bullshit.

But you already know that.

Because you like worksheets.

Which, of course, is where the idea for this book came from. Worksheets are nothing more than scaffolding and structure to creating change. It's super easy to have a great idea about making huge shifts in your life, but carrying around an idea in your back pocket, and actually having a plan in place are two entirely different things, right?

What Is This Book/Planner?

We took the topics I write about on the regular, and planned entire months around them. Rather than give you specific goals, I created tools that are designed to support your goal process in regard to these topics.

Which also means that a lot of the activities have not shown up in any of my previous books. It's mostly all new stuff. I wanted each activity to be something that you worked on throughout a period of a week, that connected with other activities within that month. So that meant a bunch of cool, new shit.

Each quarter is a season and each month is its own topic to tackle. And it all adds up to a year of hard work making badass changes. And since I've written about all of these topics in the past, you could go look for those books (along with other books on the topics I love) if you realize "this is a thing for me, I could totally do some more work in this area."

How to Use This Planner

Any way you want! Yaaay for that answer.

Seriously though, if you are trapped in the wilderness and you need to build a fire and this is the only kindling you have, no hard feelings.

Otherwise, I still say use it anyway you want. Meaning, you don't have to start at the beginning of the year. Or even the beginning of the month. Or the beginning of the book. Each month stands alone, so if you really want to tackle anxiety first off, totally switch to that month and do your thing. If you like working in order that's super cool, too. There are 54 weeks over 12 months so you've got plenty of space to spread out however you want to organize it.

Unlike the aforementioned 4th grade teacher, I don't have assignment due dates.

Unf*ck Your Year
A Weekly Unplanner and Self-Care Activity Book to Manage Your
Anxiety, Depression, Anger, Triggers, and Freak-Outs

Part of the 5-Minute Therapy series

© Faith Harper, 2020
This edition © Microcosm Publishing, 2020

First edition, first printing August 25, 2020

ISBN 9781621061816
This is Microcosm #541

Edited by Lydia Rogue
Cover and book design by Lindsey Cleworth

For a catalog, write or visit:
Microcosm Publishing
2752 N Williams Ave.
Portland, OR 97227
www.Microcosm.Pub

To join the ranks of high-class stores that feature Microcosm titles,
talk to your rep: In the U.S. Como (Atlantic), Fujii (Midwest), Book
Travelers West (Pacific), Turnaround in Europe, Manda/UTP in
Canada, New South in Australia, and GPS in Asia, India, Africa, and
South America. We are sold to the gift market by Gifts of Nature.

If you bought this on Amazon, we're so sorry because you could have gotten it
cheaper and supported a small, independent publisher at www.Microcosm.Pub

Global labor conditions are bad, and our roots in industrial
Cleveland in the 70s and 80s made us appreciate the need to treat
workers right. Therefore, our books are MADE IN THE USA.

MICROCOSM · PUBLISHING

Microcosm Publishing & Distribution focuses on the colorful, authentic, and empowering. Our books and zines have put your power in your hands since 1996, equipping readers to make positive changes in their lives and the world around them. Microcosm emphasizes skill-building, showing hidden histories, and fostering creativity. We challenge conventional publishing wisdom with books and zines about DIY skills, food, bicycling, gender, self-care, and social justice. What was once a zine distro and record label was started by Joe Biel in his bedroom and has become among the oldest independent publishing houses in Portland, Oregon.

CONTENTS

SEASON ONE

GOAL-SETTING MONTH

(Add the days of the week here.)

(Write the month in this box.)

(Fill in the date here.)

12

Goals for Goal-Setting Month

Why set goals? Because making vague ideas tangible changes our focus and sharpens our intentions. This is the month you are going to spend figuring out what you want to figure out! Isn't that meta? What do you want to hold in awareness as you start this journey?

Goals:

Write a quote, mantra or intention for the month here.

○ More Resources

Achieve Your Goals by Dr. Faith Harper

How to Be Accountable by Joe Biel and Dr. Faith Harper

MicroMOVEment Miracle Method by SARK

Align with Your Values

This activity helps us become aware of where we have fallen out of alignment with our inner compass so we can focus our efforts on reconnecting with our value system.

Circle ten adjectives that describe what you are like. Try to be as honest and accurate as possible; this is a snapshot of where you are in the present. Rank them 1–10 from most significant to least in describing your personality.

Aimless	Content	Disorganized	Hard-working	Kind	Outgoing	Sad	Strong
Anxious	Depressed	Energetic	Helpful	Lazy	Plain	Serious	Unhelpful
Careless	Disengaged	Funny	Honest	Optimistic	Purposeful	Shy	
Centered	Dishonest	Happy	Intelligent	Organized	Relaxed	Stressed	

Now pick up a different color pen and choose ten items to describe your personal ideal. Not what other people wish for you but what you truly wish for yourself. This can be difficult if you are used to letting others guide your path. So listen to your gut over your head. Now rank those ten from most to least important.

Now compare the colors. Where do they match up? Where are you out of alignment? Is any of your stuckness related to not being in alignment with your core identity?

On this week's calendar, write down the values that came to the forefront each day.

So What's the Problem, Then?

Before we can focus on solutions, we usually have to wrestle with the problem itself. We have a language that we use to define all aspects of our lives, and the language we use to define our problems can feel extra-shitty at times. Which can shut us down, effectively making problem definition our number one barrier in achieving new goals.

Define the current problem.

Cool, now highlight or underline any words that cause fear, worry, anger, or resistance from you.

Great. Now define those words. Start with "What do I mean by ..."

Review those definitions. Are they accurate? Helpful? Are there any words that are more accurate? Do any need to be redefined to be useful to your path to move forward?

Check back in with yourself. What emotional responses do you have to those words now?

SMART Goal Setting

SMART Goals allow you to create structure around your goals, so they aren't just wasting away in good intentions land. And, bonus, they help you track your progress.

Start with a goal: e.g. being healthy.

>

S — Specific. This is the who, what, where, when, and why of goal setting. In our example, the general value of being healthy turns into a specific goal of decreasing sugar consumption and working out. Now you do it:

>

M — Measurable. Making the goal measurable helps drill it down even further. The vague goal of "working out" becomes walking 2x a week and less sugar means having scrambled eggs for breakfast instead of a cinnamon roll 5x a week.

>

A — Achievable. Can you do it? How can you make sure it's worth the investment in terms of energy, effort, and cost? Maybe you can't afford a gym membership right now, so your working out goal turns into walking outside or doing 20 minutes of yoga in the house.

>

R — Relevant. This is the why of the goal . . . what's the larger objective? If exercising is a way to get a critical family member off your back, is that really relevant to you? Or is it relevant for you because it helps you have more energy? Check in with your goal: how is it relevant?

>

T — Timely. Have a timetable for the goal. You want your timeline to be reasonable and flexible. You might set a goal of eating vegetables for dinner three weeks in a month for six months. What's your timeline?

>

Letter To My Future Self

This exercise is adapted from the book *Taming the Outer Child* by Susan Anderson. I love the idea of framing the positive outcome you're aiming for *plus* taking responsibility for the work ahead. Even a really good, SMART goal is so focused on the "how" of goal setting that we forget "why" we are doing it. Here's to keeping the "why" front and center!

I feel _____ and _____ because I accomplished the following goals in the past two years: _____.

I had to overcome many difficult obstacles, including _____, _____, and even _____.

In order to overcome these obstacles, I had to practice utilizing new behaviors, including _____, _____, and _____.

While the work was primarily my own responsibility, I am grateful for the help of _____.

In the future, I look forward to achieving _____.

With Gratitude,
Me

SELF-CARE MONTH

Goals for Self-Care Month

Self-care. Ugh, one of those buzzwords that generally makes us want to throw up a bit in our mouths, right? Self-care isn't about pedicures and bubble baths (though let me be clear, I quite enjoy both). It's about keeping our body as healthy as it can be and prioritizing what we need to be as intellectually and emotionally aligned with our values as we possibly can . . . so we can handle whatever shit storms come our way.

All the activities this month are all about doing the difficult self-care work. So tell me now, what are you looking to accomplish for your badass self?

Quote, mantra or intention

Goals:

_____

_____

_____

_____

_____

More Resources
Furiously Happy by Jenny Lawson
Self-Compassion by Dr. Faith Harper
Tiny, Beautiful Things by Cheryl Strayed
Don't Just Do Something, Sit There by Sylvia Boorstein

Sit the Fuck Down

Mindfulness meditation is just about paying attention to your brain and body in a conscious way. Nothing changes until we start to really understand the nature of what needs to be changed. And that's all that mindfulness is.

If you have control over your lighting, dim the lights but don't turn them off. Don't use music for this activity, in fact the less ambient noise the better. Decide in advance how long you plan to sit and set a timer for yourself.

Sit in a position that is comfortable for you on the floor or in a chair. It's important that you are physically comfortable so your mind doesn't focus on your discomfort. You want to be relaxed but alert. Sit with your spine as erect as possible. Cast your eyes slightly down but do not close them. Do not focus on any particular object.

Then, just sit there. Don't *do* anything. Thoughts and feelings will come and go. Note them quietly in your mind as "thinking," then let them pass. Try to maintain an awareness of the movement of your breath, in and out. When your attention wanders away from your breath and into your thoughts, gently remind yourself to move back to your breath.

Try to practice your mindfulness regularly this week. Give yourself gold stars and track how it felt on the calendar on the next page.

Take Your Temperature

This week, use the calendar on the next page to take your emotional temperature every day. Try it here first, right now. Stop and notice:

What's going on in your body?

What are you thinking/imagining?

What are you feeling as a result of these thoughts? Rate the intensity of these feelings on a scale of 1 to 10.

What external shit in your life is helping you cope or making it worse?

Were any of these questions impossible to answer right now? That's okay. Just acknowledge that you aren't able to access all the parts of your experience and remind yourself that even just noticing that you feel numb is a perfectly acceptable place to start.

Remember: You have permission to feel what you feel!

Letting Go of Your Inheritance

Our inheritance is not just the ugly-ass china that our grandparents insist on passing down to us, but also the ways our family members saw the world, and how they shared their experiences. Self-care includes figuring out that emotional inheritance so we can unpack that which no longer serves us. What are the beliefs, fears, stereotypes, and habits you were led to believe were fundamental truths about you, other people, and the world in general?

Consider how your inheritance has influenced your perspective on the following topics:

Success	*Romantic Relationships/*	*Emotional and Mental*	*Money*	*Family*
Spiritual awareness	*Sex*	*Health*	*Career/Profession*	*Parenting*
Fun/Enjoyment	*Social Relationships*	*Body/Physical Health*		

Then answer the following:

What does success look like?

What constitutes a healthy relationship?

What do you believe about spirituality?

What do you believe about money?

What was the intention behind the messages you were given?

What aspects of these intentions do not serve you in the present?

How can you reframe your inheritances to serve your growth and the health of your relationships in the present and future?

This Week

Overcoming Immunity to Change

We've all had some experience where we have a plan for taking better care of ourselves but we don't achieve it. *Immunity to change* comes from our brain's way of protecting ourselves from potential failure, embarrassment, and other hurt. When we map out how we created our change immunity, it's far easier to dismantle it.

Your commitment: What is one thing that is important to you and will be a big deal in your life if you can make it happen?

Concrete barriers: What barriers are working against you achieving this goal that are in your control? What are you doing that is getting in your way? Don't explain why, just list everything that's in the way.

Competing commitments: This, not willpower, is the actual root cause of struggling with change. Look at your list of barriers and imagine doing the opposite of whatever they are. What fears come to mind?

Big assumptions: Unpack your beliefs around these fears, using "If . . . then . . . " statements.

Now, start testing these assumptions. For example, maybe your assumption is that saying no to your friends will mean they can't count on you. Argue with that. Look at all the other ways you are a reliable friend. Or ask your friends what makes you reliable. Test saying no to smaller things this week and see how people respond before you start saying no to larger things. Record the results on your weekly calendar on the next page.

Gratitude Letter

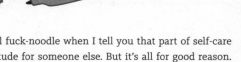

You are going to think I'm a total fuck-noodle when I tell you that part of self-care month is to reflect on your gratitude for someone else. But it's all for good reason. Focusing on gratitude helps us foster self-comfort when we feel like shit, and helps us be more compassionate to ourselves and others.

Make a list of the people you're close to who offer you comfort and security. Who is the person you most like spending time with? Who is the person you want to talk to when you are worried about something? Who is the person you turn to when you are feeling down? Who is the person you know will always be there for you? Who is the person you want to share your success with?

Write down six positive qualities that are common to these people, qualities that only they strongly embody.

Now visualize a specific situation where you were feeling distressed or worried and one of those people comforted and helped you.

Write a description of that instance and how you felt, then focus on that experience and how it's helped you be the person you are today.

Draw a heart on the calendar every time you feel gratitude for someone this week.

FINANCIAL PLANNING MONTH

Goals for Financial Planning Month

Money goals. Ugh. Even the people I know who seem to have it together about money (at least from the outside it looks like they have plenty of it) are really struggling. There are weekly activities to help you become more money-mindful, save differently, look at making more money in the short term, and think about work and career in the longer term.

What do you most want to accomplish financially this month?

Goals:

Quote, mantra or intention

More Resources

Unfuck Your Worth by Dr. Faith Harper

Finances For My Daughter by Bob Veres

Where Does It Go?

Spending money on a latte or a movie or a meal out or whatever isn't "bad" or "wrong." We need joy in our life, and if we try to erase all fun we end up feeling resentful and grumpy and are far *more* likely to fall off our budget wagon because of it. So don't think of this exercise as a way of self-shaming, but of recognition. Sometimes we are spending money without being mindful of it, and by paying attention we can make adjustments without losing the fun.

Record how much you spent and on what on the calendar to the right.

At the end of the week, reflect on the things you bought. What did you notice about your spending habits? Did they change because you were paying attention to them? (e.g., you almost bought a new shirt at Target but realized you didn't really need it and knew you would have to write it down on the log?)

What changes do you want to make based on what you noticed?

Save Money by Doing Instead of Not Doing

One of the fundamental truths about human nature is that it is always easier to start doing something than to stop doing something. Eating poorly? Add the good foods and let the less-healthy stuff find its own way out of your diet. Overly critical? Focus on saying positive things and watch the criticisms wander off on their own.

Same is true with saving money. If you are looking to cut expenses, add new purchases and activities that are free or cheaper to your day and let them naturally replace the stuff you spend money on now. This feels more like a fun challenge rather than deprivation and limitation.

My mission for you this week is to find three cost-saving activities that you can engage in as an add-on rather than as a replacement.

One:
Two:
Three:

At the end of the week, check in. Did the budget expenditure you were hoping to reduce show a decrease this week? Might it over time? Was it easier to make the switch using this method? Do you think you can carry forth this method in other ways?

The Point of Work

We can't talk about money without talking about work. I mean, generally we have to work in order to get the money we need to access the things that we need to stay alive. But there's other value associated with work beyond the paycheck we receive. And understanding our personal value system can help us make better decisions about the work we do in the present and in the future, whether it be for a day job or side hustle.

Consider the following values or rewards associated with work:

Money   *Prestige*   *Security*   *Recognition*   *Independence*

Which two rewards are your highest priorities?

Which one is the absolute lowest?

Are these priorities reflected in your current work? If not, how are they in conflict?

What would be the ideal way of getting these values back in alignment? Are any elements of this solution viable? If none, what would be a viable alternative solution?

What would be a doable first step?

Debt Repayment Plan

Alright, y'all. This week we are gonna do the thang. You are saving a little money by tracking and reducing your expenses, right? We are going to use that extra money and come up with a debt repayment plan that does not scorch you with the fire of a 1000 burning suns. Maybe 500. But definitely not 1000.

List all your unsecured debt here:

Debt	APR	Minimum Payment	Pay-Off Amount

Now, choose your payoff priorities. There are a couple of good options:

Snowball Plan: Pay as much as you can into the smallest debt first while just paying the minimum on the rest. Once that one's knocked out, you put everything you can into the next smallest one and so on. This plan works well psychologically because you see progress quickly and that's good motivation to stay on task.

Avalanche Plan: Like above but you focus on the debt that is accumulating the most interest first. This option will save you more in the long run. You don't see the payoff progress as quickly, but if you calculate the interest you are saving that may help your motivation level.

Which plan makes the most sense for you? Choose a method and then number your debts above in the order you'll be paying them off. Once each debt is paid off, come back and cross it out.

This Week

SEASON TWO

5 PERCENT BETTER

ADULTING MONTH

Goals for Adulting Month

Ugh, adulting is such a buzzword, isn't it? Like flossing, and making your bed, and learning how to change a tire. And yet, so many of us continue to struggle at being a good and authentic human in the world because that's *way* harder. Don't get me wrong, changing a tire is not easy. But being a grounded adult in the world is like changing a tire on quicksand. During a brushfire. While someone is throwing water balloons full of acid at you. That's what we mean by adulting, the hard work of being a kind, authentic engaged human being with a life of meaning. That's what we are working on this month. No checkbook balancing at all.

Think about what this kind of adulting would look like for you.

Goals:

Quote, mantra or intention

More Resources
Unfuck Your Adulting by Dr. Faith Harper
The Gifts of Imperfection by Brene Brown
Self-Compassion by Kristen Neff
How to Not Be a Dick by Sam Harper

47

What Kind of Person Do I Want to Be?

A big part of adulting is operating from your own moral center. Meaning, you act from a place that is congruent with the kind of person you want to be in the world. Even though everything we do and every interaction we have should operate from this place, we rarely think about what that really looks like (which is probably why we so often end up tilting at the wrong windmills). You can flip back to the Align with Your Values exercise (on page 14) for a reminder (and see what's changed since then).

What do you want to stand for? What do you believe in?

What personal attributes and positive characteristics do you want to demonstrate to yourself and others in the world?

How will you know when you are successfully living your values?

How will you know if you aren't?

How will you know if your priorities have changed and you need to recalibrate?

Exploring Wonder

Adulting means dealing with shit head-on, right? Sometimes making new headway into an old problem starts with getting super creative. Starting a problem-solving exploration process with the words "I wonder . . . " helps us expand beyond our more limiting beliefs and current habits of problem solving.

I wonder what I need to focus on right now?

I wonder where I have the most opportunities to grow?

I wonder how I can find more joy in my life?

I wonder how I can find more meaning in my life?

I wonder how I can express myself in new ways?

I wonder how I can connect more strongly in relationships?

I wonder what I can do differently?

I wonder about what comes next?

I wonder . . .

Self-Honesty

The human brain has such amazing capacities, it can even lie to itself. This doesn't make you an asshole. It makes you, newsflash, normal. But it also keeps you from operating at your full capacity and making changes in your life that you know, deep down, you need to make. This week I challenge you to pay attention to the stuff your brain has been hiding away from your conscious processes.

What feels too taboo to talk about?

Where am I afraid to go, in my own mind or with people I trust?

What would the people I love and trust say if they knew the full story?

Are there people who have suspicions that I'm not okay? What are they saying to me?

Am I acting as though things are more okay than they really are?

Am I afraid I have far less control than I think I have?

What would happen if I owned my truth, completely?

Does most of my energy each day go into keeping up a false appearance?

Am I behaving in ways that no longer serve me, out of habit or comfort?

What would be the consequence of no longer pretending?

Did you stumble upon a place for growth?

What would be the most difficult part of addressing this issue?

What would make doing so important for you in the long term?

Being a Badass Conversationalist

I spend a lot of time in therapy with people who are trying to figure out how to be better communicators. Practicing these skills this week in situations where there isn't much at stake will make it way less awkward when the stakes are higher (Job interview! First date!). Practice paying close attention when people talk, asking open-ended questions about what they say ("What was _____ like?"), and giving authentic compliments.

• What are some situations in the coming week in which you can challenge yourself to practice your communication skills?

• What are some things you can start a conversation about?

• What are your strengths with communicating with other people?

• How can you draw on those strengths?

Action Plan:

Place	Topic	Result
Grocery store	Compliment someone on something they're wearing	Told someone I liked their shoes, and they smiled and said thank you. I was nervous but it felt nice to make someone else feel good!

Gold Fucking Stars

You know what I miss from childhood? Gold stars. People recognizing the effort I put into something. Here's a worksheet so you can give gold stars to yourself for your healthy coping skills and everyday achievements.

Gold Fucking Star	The Thing I Tried	How I Felt Before I Tried the Thing (0-10)	How I Felt After I Tried the Thing (0-10)	My General Feelings About the Thing (0-10)
☆				
☆				
☆				
☆				
☆				
☆				
☆				
☆				
☆				

COPING SKILLS MONTH

Goals for Coping Skills Month

Think of what has been the hardest crap for you to deal with recently. Life is hard and sometimes there isn't much we can control except our own responses to what's going on. What is the stuff that gets to you the most, big or little? Write down what you want to focus on handling differently, so with all the skills you practice this month, you have an end result in mind!

Goals:

_____
_____
_____
_____
_____
_____
_____
_____
_____

Write a quote, mantra or intention for the month here.

More Resources
Coping Skills by Dr. Faith Harper
You Are Here by Jenny Lawson
How Not to Kill Yourself by Set Sytes

Stop! Grounding Time: 5 . . . 4 . . . 3 . . . 2 . . . 1

Here's a chance to check in with yourself, make sure you're in the present and not super-activated. This grounding skill engages the five senses, which are the ways we connect to and stay present with the world around us. Give it a whirl. Or a count. Semantics.

1. Notice and name (in your out-loud voice or inside-your-brain voice) five things you see around you.
2. Now notice and name off four things around you that you can touch. You don't have to actually touch them, but you are totally welcome to.
3. Now notice and name off three things that you hear.
4. Now notice two things you can smell. It's totally kosher to go find something like the soap in the bathroom or something.
5. Now notice one thing you can taste. You can go find something to taste if that's handy, but you can also just notice that you still taste your sandwich from lunch, or your toothpaste from earlier in the morning. Whatever works.

The key to good coping skills is to practice when you are *not* activated. So stop and ground yourself once every day this week, and give yourself a gold star on the calendar on the next page.

A.N.T. Attack

A.N.T stands for "automatic negative thoughts." Meaning, the shitty things we say to ourselves throughout the day every day. Paying attention to those thoughts and coming up with strategies to combat them (either with a complete replacement thought or a more balanced perspective) really serves to help stop the spiral of depression, anxiety, and plain old negative thinking and funky-ass mood development.

ANT	Replacement Thought OR More Balanced Response
"Everyone hates me"	"There are plenty of people who love me. I have family and several friends. That's my anxiety talking and I know it's utter bullshit."
"I fucked that up so bad."	"I didn't do as well on that project as I hoped, but I have a plan to do better next time and I know there are other things I do really well. Not being perfect makes me as human as everyone else."

Draw an ant on the calendar every day you practice this!

NAME that Shit

The NAME coping skill is great because you can low-key do it wherever you are without looking like a weirdo (helpful if you are stuck on public transport). It helps you tune in to what's going on so you can manage it without reacting to it. Your mission for this week is to practice NAMEing that shit. See what shifts for you by doing so, rock star.

Notice: Move from automatic pilot to awareness. Start paying attention to your breath, move that focus through the rest of your body. Remind yourself that your feeling is an experience . . . it's something you have at the moment, not something you are.

Acknowledge: Recognize and label your experience without judgement. Say to yourself, "I am experiencing the feeling of . . . " and/or "I am experiencing the sensation of . . . "

Make space for what you are experiencing in your body. Give the experience the space to run its course and wash away rather than trying to shove it down or lock it up.

Expand Awareness: Reach out to the world around you, even if your experience of unwanted feelings and sensations hasn't yet gone away. You made space for it to hang out and now you can reconnect to what's important to you and act in healthy and positive ways which keeps the feelings and sensations from having total control over you.

What did you NAME this week?

What changed about it once you NAMEd it?

HELLO, MY NAME IS...

Mood Tracker

Pay attention to your mood throughout the day every day this week. Seeing the patterns and changes can be illuminating. Check in with your mood periodically this week and record your results here. If you run out of room, you can record more moods in this week's calendar.

Day/Time	Mood	Situation	Magnitude (0–100)	Body Responses	Outward Behavior

At the end of the week look back. Any patterns you notice? What would be helpful in the future?

BOUNDARY DEVELOPMENT MONTH

Goals for Boundary Development Month

Boundaries are the edge territory of what belongs to us and what belongs to someone else. Our boundaries are the essential building blocks of our relationships. They are how we operate in the world. They are our rules of engagement. Our everyday expressions of consent.

This month, I want you to think of the places, people, and situations where you want to focus on having healthy boundaries.

Goals:

Quote, mantra or intention

More Resources

Unfuck Your Boundaries by Dr. Faith Harper
Empowered Boundaries by Cristien Storm
Unfuck Your Consent by Dr. Faith Harper

You Need More "No" in Your Life (and More Cowbell)

I don't know anyone who couldn't stand to have a little more "no" in their life. This week, practice saying "no." Not with willy-nilly dickitude, but thoughtfully.

When someone asks you to do a thing, ask yourself the following questions:

Yes   No

☐   ☐   Are you willing? Is this something you want to do or feel like you should do? Is there meaning in this activity for you?

☐   ☐   Are you available? And I don't mean you are running a marathon or anything, but did you have that time set aside for something else? If you planned on being home that evening to catch up on laundry, that is something on your schedule!

☐   ☐   Is there any extra information that would sway your decision to yes? Like, did you have laundry planned but a friend has Hozier tickets?

If the answer is "no" to all of the above, say it. You can say it nicely (my go-to is "I don't have the bandwidth to take that on right now but thanks for thinking of me!"), but say it firmly.

Where did you say "no" this week?

How was it received?

What was your experience of it?

Write a big "NO!" on this week's calendar every time you said a thoughtful no!

NO!

Hold Your Boundaries FAST

FAST is a dialectical behavioral therapy acronym that is used to help folks with interpersonal effectiveness. Meaning, better relationships with others. Your mission this week is to try the FAST approach when you feel your boundaries being challenged.

F: Be fair. We all have our own biases. But try to relate to the fact that it's happening. Ask yourself how the other person is seeing the situation and what their biases might be. How can you negotiate in a way that reflects the desires of everyone involved and the compromises that everyone makes are as equal as possible.

A: Don't apologize. You are allowed to have a differing opinion, and you don't have to apologize for it. You can have your opinion and still empathize with other people's opinion without labeling yourself as "wrong."

S: Stick to your values. You know what your moral center is; don't lose it in the face of negotiations with others. Being fair means owning and centering your values. What values do you need to stay true to when communicating with others?

T: Be truthful. Stay honest. Like with yourself, and with others. White lies don't serve the greater good in the long term. You can be honest without being a dick about it.

What situations did you employ FAST in?

What did you notice about how you managed your boundaries when doing so?

Draw a little running stick figure on this week's calendar every time you use this skill!

Boundaries Learned

You've heard the expression that all relationships (and not just romantic ones) teach us something . . . even if the lesson is 100% what *not* to do in the future. The important thing is to pay attention to that lesson. This is hard to do when recalling a fucked up situation activates emotional pain. But you can do the tough work so you are prepared to hold better boundaries in the future, right?

When I reflect on a past relationship in which I was deeply hurt, I can identify my part in this pain. How did I withhold love from a partner or from myself in order to meet their demands?

What lessons did I learn from these behaviors/interactions that I will use to inform my choices in the future?

How do I demonstrate those lessons in present and future relationships?

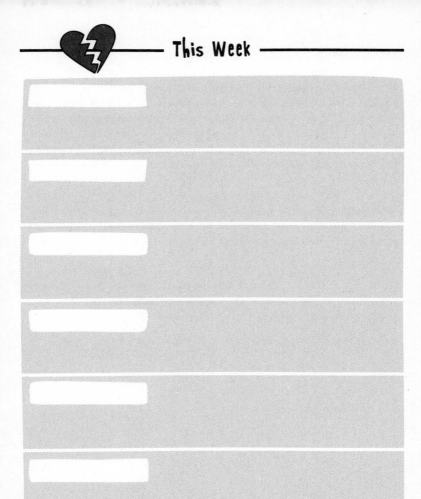

Red Flags/Green Flags

We talk about red flags around boundary violations all the time, but rarely look at the green flags in comparison. Recognizing the signs of someone who is likely trustworthy is just as important as recognizing the signs of someone who isn't.

Think about occasions where individuals demonstrated to you that they either respect your boundaries or were unwilling to do so. Or, situations you have witnessed with others.

Also consider expanding your green flags list with ideal behaviors, even if you haven't witnessed them yet. This helps you think about the kind of people you want to be on the lookout for in your life so you can nurture relationships with them!

Red Flags	Green Flags
Argues with you when you say you don't want to do something	Expresses disappointment but respects your answer
Interrogates you about your boundaries	Asks questions to better understand your experience

Learning Your Body's Responses

Try this exercise with another person. The point is to practice learning how your body responds when you agree to something that you don't really want to do, *and* when you decline to do something you really *do* want to do. It helps you discover your boundaries within your physical body by listening to the cues. Take note of your reactions and write them down below.

Come up with things that you do and don't want to do with the person you are practicing with. Steer away from anything awful or triggering. Touch can be involved but doesn't have to be. Instead, you can try it with borrowing/using something that belongs to you, or getting closer in someone's space without actually touching.

Practice saying "yes" when you mean it as well as when you don't mean it. Then the same with "no." What happens in your body each time?

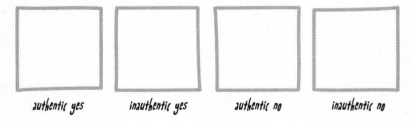

authentic yes   inauthentic yes   authentic no   inauthentic no

Did you have any "I don't know/I'm not sure/Maybe/I feel confused" experiences? What did those feel like?

SEASON THREE

MENTAL HEALTH

ANXIETY MANAGEMENT MONTH

Goals for Anxiety Management Month

I swear, anyone who says they are anxiety-free is either a liar or an extraterrestrial. If you are neither, I would love to hear your secret! Honestly, tho. Anxiety is just our brain rehearsing for all the terrible things that we think might happen. Our brains run away from us in that regard and we lose control of our reactions to the stories our brains start telling us. This month we are going to work on keeping those stories from defining and controlling our existence.

You with me? Drop your anxiety management goals here.

Goals:

Quote, mantra or intention

More Resources
This Is Your Brain on Anxiety by Dr. Faith Harper
First We Make the Beast Beautiful by Sarah Wilson

83

Positive Projection

So much of anxiety is a rehearsal for worst-case scenarios and what-ifs. It's how humans try out ideas in our minds. We don't want to lose that capability, it's really valuable. But it turns into anxiety when it's a constant loop and it triggers an idea of "not-enoughness." Meaning we don't trust our ability to do the best we can in situations, or believe that we will somehow fail ourselves or others. Managing anxiety also means learning to trust our capacity to respond to the world in ways that are important to us.

One of the ways we can do that is through projection. Projection simply means seeing in someone else something that is present within ourselves. We think of projection in a negative way, thanks to Freud. But let's explore the positives.

Write the name of someone who has qualities you admire (it can be someone you know, or a fictional character, whatever.)

Name: _____

What specific qualities do you admire about them?

Now look in the mirror and read this aloud to yourself adding the words "I am . . . " ahead of each quality you admire. Pay attention to how saying these things affects you. What do you notice in your body? What do you feel? What thoughts do you experience?

Which projection did you react to most strongly? Which reactions surprised you the most?

This Week ———————

Bee Breathing (Brahmari Pranayama)

This is a form of yogic breathing that is shown to be effective for managing anxiety. It's called bee breathing (brahmari means bee in Sanskrit, easy enough) because of the buzzing sound you make on the exhale.

Managing anxiety better means finding good tools and practicing them before your anxiety is through the roof so you can figure out which ones resonate with you. If they are secure in your toolbox, they become way easier to use when your anxiety starts acting a fool. So practice this technique this week, get a hang of it, and see if it should belong permanently in your toolbox.

Sit comfy, keep your back straight but your shoulders relaxed. Take a few natural breaths to settle yourself and close your eyes (unless that tends to activate your anxiety). Keeping your lips closed, inhale through your nostrils. Now exhale, making a humming sound with your vocal cords (like the letter "M," but without opening your mouth and enunciating the letter).

Try to make your exhale longer than your inhale (this is the big trick for calming your anxiety response), but don't do it in an unnatural, forced way (because that will make your anxiety worse and that definitely is not a good thing).

Draw a little bee on this week's calendar every time you practice your brahmari.

Retraining Anxiety through Exposure

A lot of anxiety management is practicing doing the shit that scares us so we can retrain our brains that horrible things aren't going to happen. The therapy term for that is "prolonged exposure" and this is something you can practice in manageable increments. I'm totally serious when I say manageable increments, okay? Forward progress in big leaps usually ends up in tripping and falling. Baby steps all the way!

Name your fear: _____

What specifically are you afraid of?

On a scale of 1–10, how anxious do you predict you'll be when you face your fear?

1   2   3   4   5   6   7   8   9   10

What benefit will you get out of facing your fear?

Now try exposing yourself to your fear a little bit this week. Make notes on the calendar of what you did and experienced, and rate your anxiety from 1–10.

At the end of the week, reflect on your experiences here.

How did reality compare to what your anxiety was telling you would happen?

How did you rank your anxiety vs. what you predicted would happen?

Draw a tiny monster on this week's calendar every time you face your fear!

Exceptions to Anxiety

There's a little trick in solution-focused therapy that is super helpful: focus on when there are exceptions to the problem that someone is experiencing. In this case, we are looking for exceptions to anxiety. Or, at least, times where it was far more manageable. I have worked with so many people who have developed wonderful anxiety management plans by figuring out what their anxiety-exceptions are.

Answer the following questions, starting with the center:

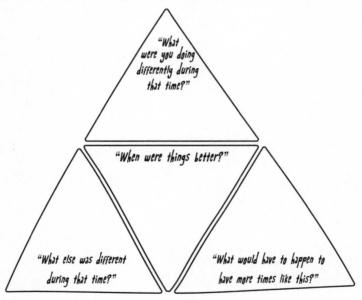

This week, every time you notice yourself *not* reacting from a place of anxiety, give yourself a high five and draw a heart on the calendar.

This Week

ANGER MANAGEMENT MONTH

Goals for Anger Management Month

In my book *Unfuck Your Anger*, I talk a lot about how anger is a secondary emotion. Meaning, it's the result of our body energetically getting ready to deal with something it's determined to be a problem.

Anger is such a difficult one. There are so many moving parts to contend with if we are trying to manage our anger. Cultural issues, other mental health issues, the things that are triggering our anger to begin with. What are you trying to figure out and have a new relationship with in regard to your anger?

Goals:

Quote, mantra or intention

More Resources
Unfuck Your Anger by Dr. Faith Harper
Don't Bite the Hook: Finding Freedom from Anger, Resentment, and Other Destructive Emotions by Pema Chödrön
Why We Snap by Douglas Fields

Unpacking Your Anger History

Anger can come from many different sources. Figuring out your specific anger patterns makes it easier to manage them.

Is your anger symptomatic of mental health, physical health, or substance use issues that you experience?

Is anger a habit for you? Has it become your go-to emotional response?

Did you learn your anger from others? Is it how your family, friends, or greater community expressed themselves when you were growing up? Or now?

Were you treated with anger by others growing up? Are you treated with anger by others now?

Are you under a lot of stress currently that you don't feel much control over?

Do you feel your anger coming on or do you just go kaboom and it surprises you?

What did you notice in answering these questions? What are some potential ways to manage your anger based on these realizations?

The Continuous You

This is a super-simple version of a classic exercise from Acceptance and Commitment Therapy. It works well for all kinds of strong feelings. I'm including it here because anger is near the top of the list of emotions that are considered something we "are" instead of something we "have."

This week when you find yourself feeling angry (or even the more mild forms of anger like frustration or irritability), try the following:

Notice what you're feeling. Give the emotion a label (agitated, pissed off, livid).

Now remind yourself that you are noticing this feeling.

And if you are noticing it, it means it's something that you are experiencing, not something that you are.

Remind yourself that what you are noticing changes frequently throughout the week, but the you who is doing the noticing remains the same. Which means your moods do not define you, right?

What did you notice frequently through this week?

What feelings/words are attached to that?

How have your feelings changed for noticing them?

Put an angry scribble on this week's calendar every time you notice your anger. Make the scribble as intense as your feeling.

Bias Disruptors

The brain has multiple shortcuts it takes to make decisions more quickly and preserve energy. These shortcuts often serve us well, but when they fail we can get stuck in unhelpful thinking (and subsequent behavior) patterns. This week, look at how three biases might be affecting your interactions, especially when they activate frustration and anger within you.

For each bias, write down an example of a time you fell prey to it and how you felt under its sway.

Availability Bias: Our likelihood of believing something just because the idea is readily available.

Confirmation Bias: When we seek out data that supports what we already believe.

Hindsight Bias: When we think we are better at predicting the future than we are by deciding we "saw something coming" when we actually didn't.

Every time you notice biased thinking in yourself this week, draw a little scale on the calendar.

This Week

Personalizing Your Anger Experiences

Choose a time in the last week that you got really angry, and reflect on these questions:

What are the underlying roots of your anger? If you aren't sure, reflect on when you first noticed that you were angry. What was going on around you? What were you doing, thinking, or remembering?

Once you figured out these underlying roots, are they legit or are they more about you and your history than about the present situation?

If the roots are legit, do they need to be addressed or is it one of those bullshit daily life things that just happens?

If it needs to be addressed, what is the best way to do so? How do you correct the situation with as little disruption as possible?

What can you do to keep from getting further hurt in the process (physically, emotionally, and mentally)?

Can you keep the hurt to others minimal (physically, mentally, and emotionally)?

Does it need to be addressed immediately, or can it wait until you are calmer and feel safer?

Is there anyone you can talk to who is going to have a healthy, supportive perspective, but also totally call you out on your shit if need be?

After you act (instead of react), then evaluate the results. Did it work? Is this a strategy that you can use again? Are you still angry or are you feeling better and safer now?

AHEN in Practice

AHEN stands for Anger comes from Hurt, Expectations not met, and/or Needs not met.

Now that you've learned about the root of your anger, this week I want you to notice when you are angry and figure out which HENs are creating that anger.

Situation	HEN	Specifics of the Underlying HEN
My spouse didn't do the dishes	Expectations Not Met	I wasn't hurt and it wasn't a real need, but I had expected to just get started with cooking and I felt disappointed and inconvenienced.

Draw a little chicken on this week's calendar every time you think through your HENs.

TRAUMA MANAGEMENT MONTH

Goals for Trauma Management Month

You knew it was coming, though, right? I don't know anyone who hasn't been scarred by trauma. And when I say *trauma* I mean anything that overwhelms our ability to cope.

And doing the work to be better is some of the hardest mental health work to do. You don't have to be experiencing PTSD to see the effects of trauma on emotional wellness. And everyone deserves proper space to heal trauma. And now you are an old hat at this, so you barely need me to prompt you to think about how your trauma history is impacting the present, and decide what issues you want to focus on this month. Let's do the thing.

Goals:

quote, mantra or intention

More Resources
Unfuck Your Brain by Dr. Faith Harper
Waking the Tiger by Peter Levine
Trauma Stewardship by Laura Lipsky
Trauma Sensitive Mindfulness by David A. Treleaven

Create Your Present Story

A trigger is something in the present that activates our past trauma. For example, a car brake squealing can make the brain freak out and think you are getting hit by a car again. That's why creating a narrative about your safety in the present moment can help you stay in the present in the face of triggers.

One of the most powerful tools for staying grounded in the present is storytelling. Write yourself a new story of present safety here. You can use statements such as "In the past I was a victim, now I am a survivor" or "I have the tools I need to keep myself safe in the present, I am surrounded by people who love me." You may want to carry a copy of this story with you to refer to in tense situations.

Grounding Skills Checklist

Grounding may seem like a complicated thing, but in reality all it refers to is our ability to maintain our mental awareness of the here and now. To stay in the present and in our bodies. It's the opposite of dissociation, which is a huge struggle for those of us in trauma recovery.

There are three categories of grounding skills and a billion (or at least several) ideas that fit into each of them. The goal of this week is to try out new ones and find out which ones work best for you. The 5, 4, 3, 2, 1 exercise from Coping Month is a great grounding skill. Experiment with at least one new skill every day. I'm adding a few of each to get you started, and endless more are just a google search away. Highlight your favorites at the end of the week to use again.

Physical Grounding	Soothing Grounding	Mental Grounding
Run cool water over your wrists	Splash water on your face	Stand barefoot in the grass

Every time you try a grounding skill this week, draw a little flower on this week's calendar.

Types of Triggers

There are three different ways of being activated by a trauma reminder. This week, I encourage you to pay attention when you are trauma-activated as to what type of trigger you're experiencing. This information will help you figure out better ways to recover.

True Triggers: That pre-thought wordless terror. It's a body based felt sense reaction that we often don't even recognize until after the fact. The best way to handle a true trigger is to simply notice its existence.

Distressing Reminders: Things that call up memories of the trauma and cause awful feelings but our prefrontal cortex remains mostly online. A lot of times we can describe what we are feeling even if we can't explain it. The best way to handle a distressing reminder is to soothe yourself when you are experiencing it.

Uncomfortable Associations: These occur when something that would otherwise be pleasant or at least neutral has an association to our trauma. We are able to manage these associations by consciously reframing them.

Record your triggers here:

True Trigger	Distressing Reminders	Uncomfortable Associations

Trigger Response Plan

Now that you have an idea about the different types of triggers you are experiencing, you can create a plan to manage them based on their specific level of douche-baggery. This week, I want you to try using coping and grounding skills that are specific to your types of triggers and rate how they worked so you can start to develop a more specific plan of attack for dealing with them.

Trigger	Trigger Type	Trigger Management Skill	Effectiveness

SEASON FOUR

BODY

BODY POSITIVITY MONTH

Goals for Body Positivity Month

We live in a capitalistic society that benefits greatly from us hating our bodies. What would happen if we started shifting to more self-acceptance? I can't think of a more powerful political revolution, can you? What aspects of body positivity do you want to focus on this month?

Goals:

Quote, mantra or intention

More Resources

The Body Is Not an Apology by Sonja Rene Taylor
Healthy at Every Size by Linda Bacon
52 Ways to Love Your Body by Kimber Simpkins
Detox Your Masculinity by Aaron Sapp and Dr. Faith Harper

My Body Positivity Reboot Plan

First things first: come up with a plan. What does body positivity look like to you? What changes do you want to see in your body? I've added some suggestions here, but they're only a starting point for you to create your own. Write your ideals here to create your own body positivity manifesto:

1. I wear clothes that fit properly (not too tight, not too loose) and that I feel comfortable and authentic wearing.
2. I don't follow (or at least I mute) social media accounts that make me feel bad about myself.
3. I engage in forms of exercise that are not designed to change the shape of my body, but help me feel good, healthy, and strong. And only stuff that's *fun*.
4.

5.

6.

7.

8.

9.

10.

Body Safety Map

We have a culture of mind-body disconnect. And that's fucked up and toxic. If we aren't aware of what's going on in our bodies, how will we ever begin to understand our emotional reactions? Safe and grounded starts in the body.

Scan your body to figure out which areas feel safe and secure for you and which tend to get activated when you are stressed. For example, I feel stress in my stomach; others feel it in their neck and shoulders.

Now scan again for what parts of your body feel safe and calm.

Use the following color codes to mark the body map, and make notes too if you'd like.

Red – The places that feel high-range activated
Orange – The places that feel medium-range activated
Yellow – The places that feel low-range activated
Green – The places that feel neutral
Blue – The places that feel calm

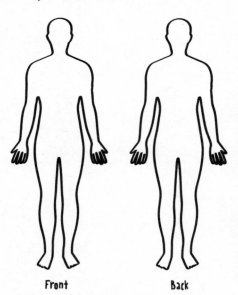

Every day this week, spend a few minutes sitting quietly and moving your awareness back and forth between the stress-activated parts of your body and the calm, safe parts.

Draw a cool blue dot on the calendar for every day you try this exercise.

The Inner Message Triad

Our relationship with our bodies is a complicated one. No one feels 100% amazing or awful about themselves. Most of us have things we like, things we really don't like, and things that just exist as neither positive or negative. Before we move on to making some shifts, take some time this week to list out your positives, negatives, and neutral feelings about your body and/or parts of your body.

Positives	Neutral	Negatives

Draw a plus sign in the calendar every time you catch yourself noticing something you like about your body this week.

The Negativity Reframe

This week, I want you to focus on noticing when the negative body messages come up and practice reframing them to neutral. It's okay if you don't love yourself perfectly. That shit is hard. But if you can create at least a neutrality treaty with these issues you will have a lot more peace and emotional energy. This week, come up with some good cognitive reframes and try them out. Which ones are the most helpful that you can continue to use?

Negative	*Neutral*

Social Media Detox Week

This week, I want you to focus on limiting the amount of time you spend on social media. That shit can be toxic to your self-image because you're constantly comparing yourself to others, even subconsciously. And it makes it hard to tune into your body. Plus then you'll have more time to do other things in life (like get through your to-be-read pile).

Day One: Pay attention to the number of times you pick up/open up/use your phone, tablet, or laptop, etc. during the day.

Day Two: Yesterday's number? Cut that in half. THE PAINNNNNNN!

Day Three: Eat all meals and snacks mindfully, instead of scrolling on your phone, tablet, laptop while eating.

Day Four: No phone for the first 45 minutes after waking up.

Day Five: No social media scrolling for two hours before bedtime.

Day Six: Call someone you usually only connect with on social media or by text. Scary, I knooooow! But hey, even just leaving them a message like "I saw the picture from your fishing trip online and realized we haven't chatted in forever and I would love to catch up!"

Day Seven: REFLECT. What is your relationship with your own body today? Any changes just by making some small detox changes? Anything you want to make a habit?

Draw a heart on this week's calendar every day you try one of these goals, and draw radiant lines around it every time you succeed.

SLEEP MASTERY MONTH

Goals for Sleep Mastery Month

Sleep is absolutely necessary for our survival. Our sleep quality affects every part of our lives, from our mental and physical health to our relationships. If your sleep is awesome you probably aren't even looking at this section. So it's currently less than awesome. What's a reasonable measure of making it more awesome? More sleep? Better quality? Figuring out how it got so fucked to begin with? Throw those goals down here!

Goals:

Quote, mantra or intention

More Resources

Unfuck Your Sleep by Dr. Faith Harper

Why We Sleep by Matthew Walker

The Sleep Revolution by Arianna Huffington

Sleep Tracker

This week I just want you to track your sleep. If you have a fitbit or other tracking device, that's awesome. If not, the SleepCycle app is free for thirty days then only $1 a year after that.

On the facing calendar, record how many hours you slept each day (and which hours). Make a note of if you consumed alcohol or other drugs, or if you exercised that day. Rate the quality of your sleep from 1–10.

After the end of the week, reflect on any patterns you notice here.

When do you sleep best?

How much sleep do you get on average?

What affected your sleep patterns? (Some common ones are exercise, food, drugs, alcohol, caffeine, and stress.)

Now try tracking your sleep all month and see what changes.

Detox the Sleep Fuckery

I go into detail about why all of these tips will greatly increase your chances of improving your sleep in my zine *Unfuck Your Sleep*. This is the basic list format so you have a single resource for focusing your energy on improving your sleep this week. Keep track of which tips you utilized on which days (and you can totally keep tracking your sleep like you did last week to start looking at the difference).

* Lower the temperature in your room
* Cut out alcohol
* Cut out cannabis
* Avoid caffeine and nicotine before bed
* Skip the evening nap
* Try melatonin or tryptophan a few hours before you hit the sack
* Don't watch TV in bed
* Use blue light blocking glasses in the evening
* Use a blue-blocking app on your laptop or desktop
* Get some sunlight during the day
* Exercise during the day
* Use a weighted blanket
* Drink chamomile or banana peel tea
* Give yourself 30 minutes to fall asleep once you get in bed. If you are tossing and turning, do something else until you feel sleepy and try again.

Caffeine Log

Don't get me wrong, I consider caffeine a hug from a good friend. I also happen to think it's a consistent issue for people trying to get better sleep. I don't drink my beloved coffee after 2PM unless I know I'm intentionally staying up late for something (and even then, I do half-caff). Making that change made a huge impact in the quality of my sleep. This week, I want you to log your caffeine intake and work in the upcoming weeks to start decreasing it. Aim for 10% less per week during the 6 hours before bedtime until you have your system cleared out.

A few of the common caffeine amounts are listed here, but you should also be able to find the info if you run a quick internet search on your favorite beverage (assuming it's not in a can where you can read the amount on the back). Add your favorite sources of caffeine here too.

Source	Amount
8 oz Drip Coffee	95 mg
8 oz Black Tea	47 mg
8 oz Green Tea	30–50 mg
1 oz Dark Chocolate	12 mg

On this week's calendar, track how much caffeine you consume each day and what time—and then what time you went to bed.

Kapalbhati (Pursed Lip) Breathing

This form of breathing reduces excess carbon dioxide in the body, improves ventilation, and calms the vagal nerve . . . all of which help with sleep. If you have found that getting your brain to shut the fuck up once you lay down is the hard part, see if doing this breathing exercise makes a difference.

Breathe in deeply through your nose like you are smelling something yummy.

Purse your lips like you are going to blow bubbles

Through your pursed lips, exhale three times more slowly than you inhaled.

Repeat until you start to feel sleepy.

How did you feel after trying this technique?

What differences did you see in your sleep quality from the week before?

How has your sleep quality changed over the course of this month?

Draw some pursed lips on this week's calendar for every day you try this exercise.

INTIMACY DEVELOPMENT MONTH

Goals for Intimacy Development Month

Intimacy can mean soooo many different things. We think about romantic partner intimacy, but it's far bigger than that. You will notice the activities for this month are not specific to romantic partners. So they are totally doable for any close relationships. So, hey, anywhere you want to make some relationship improvement *or* any place you want to make some self-improvement so you have healthier relationships in the future? It all works this month. Kick off this month by listing your goals here.

Goals:

Quote, mantra or intention

More Resources

Unfuck Your Intimacy by Dr. Faith Harper

Mating in Captivity by Esther Perel

Sexual Intelligence by Marty Klein

Relationship Inventory

Oftentimes in our day to day interactions, we lose sight of the "bigger picture." This is an opportunity to see your relationship or friendship with someone else in its entirety. Does it operate in a nourishing way for the both of you? Are there issues that can and should be resolved?

Name of the other person _____

The nature of our relationship _____

What I expect from this other person _____
_____

What I get from this other person _____
_____

What the other person expects from me _____
_____

What the other person gets from me _____
_____

What's working well for me in this relationship _____
_____
_____

What is currently problematic for me in this relationship _____
_____
_____

What would be the ideal resolution of this problem? _____
_____
_____

Is this something that is achievable? If so, how would you start? If it's not achievable, is it something you can compromise on in order to maintain the relationship? Why or why not? _____
_____
_____

Relational Images

Relational images are how we expect other people to react to us. They are things we consider to be core truths about the world. Whether or not they are empirically true, we operate like they are. Which means that these rules we create about our relationships can hold us down from living a fulfilling and authentic life more than anything else because we are always so worried about how others will respond to our authenticity. Ask yourself the same question and see if anything comes up for you in the same way.

If I say . . . _____
Other people will . . . _____

If I say . . . _____
Other people will . . . _____

If I say . . . _____
Other people will . . . _____

If I say . . . _____
Other people will . . . _____

What surprised you doing this exercise?

Did you uncover some "truths" that you didn't realize you were operating from?

How are they affecting your relationships?

What do you want to focus on changing?

I See, I Imagine

This is a great activity to separate fact from fantasy. I'm not saying that with my judgy pants on—we *all* do this thing where we create a story about a relationship we are excited about and fail to recognize what's our story and what's the current reality. Getting re-grounded in reality (versus all the possible futures we are envisioning) can help us make better relationship navigation decisions.

When I reflect on (a relationship/situation) . . .

I see (list only concrete facts) . . .

I imagine (list hopes, fantasies about what is true about this situation now or in the future) . . .

Do you like what you imagine more than what you currently see? Is it time to make a change in this situation?

Objective Effectiveness

Objective effectiveness is a term used in dialectical behavioral therapy to break down how we can best get what we want in a relationship. The acronym DEAR MAN is a great mnemonic for remembering the best ways to be effective without being a manipulative shithead.

For each letter in the acronym, write down an example of when you used it this week and how it made you feel.

Describe: Clearly and concretely say what you want. Even people who know us super well don't read minds, you know?

Express: Share your emotions while taking responsibility for them. "I feel . . . when you . . . " is far more effective than "you made me mad."

Assert: Being assertive isn't dickitude, it's honesty. "I don't know if I'm feeling up to it" is a hint, but "I'm exhausted and want to skip the party this evening" is assertive.

Reinforce: When people do the thing you ask them to do, thank them!

Mindful: Don't get sidetracked by off-topic disagreements. Stick to what issue you are trying to resolve.

Appearance: Demonstrate confidence in how you present yourself. Even if your words are assertive, people are less likely to take you seriously if your body language isn't.

Negotiate: Be open to compromise—relationships are give and take.

This Week

Lessons Learned

One of the other therapist-y things I say on the regular is "we either win or we learn." No one hits it out of the park every time, right? We all have things we don't succeed at, and relationships that don't work out. What really gets us in trouble is when we make the same mistakes over and over again . . . just with different people each time. Taking the time to see our patterns is the best way to avoid them.

When I reflect on a past relationship in which I was deeply hurt, can I identify my part in this pain? How did I withhold love from a partner or from myself?

What lessons did I learn from these behaviors/interactions that I will use to inform my choices in the future?

This Week

EMERGENCY AND IMPORTANT CONTACTS

Name: _____

Phone #: _____

Email Address: _____

Mailing Address: _____

_____

Social Media Handles: _____

Name: _____

Phone #: _____

Email Address: _____

Mailing Address: _____

_____

Social Media Handles: _____

Name: _____

Phone #: _____

Email Address: _____

Mailing Address: _____

_____

Social Media Handles: _____

Name: _____

Phone #: _____

Email Address: _____

Mailing Address: _____

Social Media Handles: _____

Name: _____

Phone #: _____

Email Address: _____

Mailing Address: _____

Social Media Handles: _____

Name: _____

Phone #: _____

Email Address: _____

Mailing Address: _____

Social Media Handles: _____

Name: _____

Phone #: _____

Email Address: _____

Mailing Address: _____

Social Media Handles: _____

National Suicide Hotline 1-800-273-8255

MENSTRUATION TRACKER

Day	1	2	3	4	5	6	7	8	9	10	11	12	13	14
JANUARY														
FEBRUARY														
MARCH														
APRIL														
MAY														
JUNE														
JULY														
AUGUST														
SEPTEMBER														
OCTOBER														
NOVEMBER														
DECEMBER														

☐ Spotting   ☐ Light flow   ☐ Medium flow

☐ Heavy flow   ☐ Cramps   ☐ _____

(Color in boxes to create personalized color code.)

(Add additional symptoms you want to track.)

15	16	17	18	19	20	21	22	23	24	25	26	27	28	29	30	31

☐ _____   ☐ _____   ☐ _____
☐ _____   ☐ _____   ☐ _____

MEDICATION TRACKER

Pharmacy:		Pharmacy:	
Phone #:		Phone #:	
Address:		Address:	
Medication:		Medication:	
Dose:	Freq:	Dose:	Freq:
Date:	Time:	Date:	Time:
Doctor:		Doctor:	
Side effects:		Side effects:	
Notes:		Notes:	

Medication:		Medication:	
Dose:	Freq:	Dose:	Freq:
Date:	Time:	Date:	Time:
Doctor:		Doctor:	
Side effects:		Side effects:	
Notes:		Notes:	

Medication:		Medication:	
Dose:	Freq:	Dose:	Freq:
Date:	Time:	Date:	Time:
Doctor:		Doctor:	
Side effects:		Side effects:	
Notes:		Notes:	

Medication:		Medication:	
Dose:	Freq:	Dose:	Freq:
Date:	Time:	Date:	Time:
Doctor:		Doctor:	
Side effects:		Side effects:	
Notes:		Notes:	

Medication:		Medication:	
Dose:	Freq:	Dose:	Freq:
Date:	Time:	Date:	Time:
Doctor:		Doctor:	
Side effects:		Side effects:	
Notes:		Notes:	

Medication:		Medication:	
Dose:	Freq:	Dose:	Freq:
Date:	Time:	Date:	Time:
Doctor:		Doctor:	
Side effects:		Side effects:	
Notes:		Notes:	

Medication:		Medication:	
Dose:	Freq:	Dose:	Freq:
Date:	Time:	Date:	Time:
Doctor:		Doctor:	
Side effects:		Side effects:	
Notes:		Notes:	

ABOUT THE AUTHOR

Faith G. Harper, PhD, LPC-S, ACS, ACN is a bad-ass, funny lady with a PhD. She's a licensed professional counselor, board supervisor, certified sexologist, and applied clinical nutritionist with a private practice and consulting business in San Antonio, TX. She has been an adjunct professor and a TEDx presenter, and proudly identifies as a woman of color and uppity intersectional feminist. She is the author of the book *Unf*ck Your Brain* and many other popular zines and books on subjects such as anxiety, depression, and grief. She is available as a public speaker and for corporate and clinical trainings.

EVEN MORE READING FOR CARING ABOUT YOURSELF AT WWW.MICROCOSM.PUB:

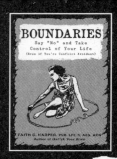